Explore the Outdoors

Kayaking

Have Fun, Be Smart

by Allison Stark Draper

Rosen Publishing Group, Inc.
New York

For Stark

Published in 2000 by The Rosen Publishing Group, Inc.
29 East 21st Street, New York, NY 10010

Copyright © 2000 by The Rosen Publishing Group, Inc.

First Edition

Library of Congress Cataloging-in-Publication Data

Draper, Allison Stark.
    Kayaking : have fun, be smart / by Allison Stark Draper.
        p. cm. — (Explore the outdoors)
    Includes bibliographical references and index.
    Summary: Describes the sport of kayaking, the equipment and gear needed,
maneuvers, and safety.
    ISBN 0-8239-3166-8
    1. Kayaking—Juvenile literature. [1. Kayaks and kayaking.] I. Title. II. Series.
GV784.3 .D72 2000
797.1'224—dc21   99-057242
                                                                                 CIP
                                                                                 AC

Manufactured in the United States of America

Contents

Introduction: The Thrill of the Kayak

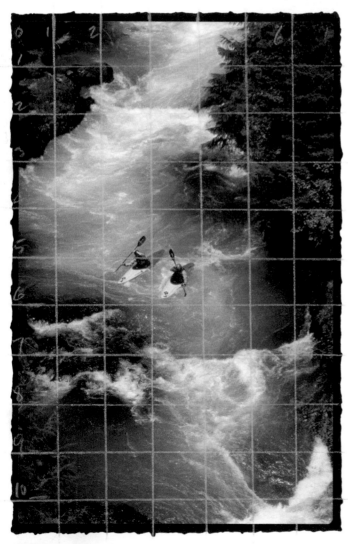

White water!

Imagine yourself shooting down a narrow canyon of foaming white water, surging up on a heavy, silky ocean swell, or simply sitting in a boat little more than twice your height, magically suspended on a flat blue sheet of water under a huge blue dome of sky. This is kayaking.

People say that the greatest modern thrill is speed—cars, motorcycles, jet planes, rockets. One of the best ways to get going fast is in one of the oldest boats on the planet: the kayak. One of the nice things about kayaking, unlike, say, drag racing, is that you don't have to be a highly trained professional to do it. You simply visit your local boat club and sign up for a few lessons. Before you know it, you'll be skimming through the water as if you were born to it.

The History of the Kayak

The kayak is probably eight or nine thousand years old. It was developed by the Inuit peoples of the Arctic for survival in the harsh seas of their homeland. They made their kayaks of driftwood and sealskin and used them for hunting, fishing, and transportation.

Kayaking for fun is a totally modern concept. When the Europeans learned about kayaking in the early twentieth century, they started to build their own versions out of

People have been kayaking for eight thousand years.

5

bamboo and sailcloth. They used them as adventure boats. By the middle of the century, European kayaks had crossed the English Channel, traveled from Germany to India, and skimmed the icy shores of the North and South Poles.

The early "foldaboats," or collapsible kayaks, made their first appearance at the Olympics in 1936. In the 1950s, rigid fiberglass boats became standard due to the superior lightness, strength, and durability of fiberglass. In the 1980s—just in time for extreme sports—boat makers introduced the plastic kayak, fondly referred to by boaters as "Tupperware."

The Modern Kayaker

Plastic kayaks are almost impossible to damage. This means that kayakers—once they get good—can pretty much go crazy. And they do! Kayakers, as a breed, tend to be dedicated to pushing the envelope. In recent years the record for the vertical run of a natural waterfall (just paddling your boat to the top of the falls and plunging down) has risen to 78 feet.

Of course, you don't have to be crazy to love to kayak. One of the best things about kayaking is how much fun it is at every skill and comfort level. There is almost no waiting time between first getting into a boat and really beginning to enjoy yourself. If you aren't a natural thrill-seeker, you'll find that there are few things as pleasurable as letting a casual river suck you along or a lazy ocean swell beneath you while you admire the scenery. From the dense woodland of hilly Tennessee to the sheer red bluffs of the Grand Canyon to the pale icy water of northern Canada and the Arctic, nothing brings you closer to the real world than a kayak.

Kayaking is an exhilarating and challenging sport.

1 The Inuit "Hunter's Boat"

"Kayak" means "hunter's boat." For thousands of years, the Inuit peoples of Greenland and northern Canada have used kayaks to hunt. The Inuit (sometimes called Eskimos) may have invented the kayak, or they may have refined an earlier boat of the Aleuts, a people who crossed the Bering Strait from Asia to Alaska in 7000 BC.

The Arctic shoreline of Canada, where the Inuit made their home, is mostly water. Cold, black inlets separate barren points of land. Flat sheets of ice stretch far out into the sea. The weather is bitter, the summers are short, and the land is poor. Rather than grow and harvest crops, the Inuit hunted animals for fur and meat.

The Inuit used their kayaks to hunt caribou, waterfowl, sea otter, and seal. It is hard for a slow-moving human to surprise these animals on foot or chase them into the sea. In a swift and silent kayak, a hunter could sneak up on an animal and kill it with a kind of spear called a harpoon.

Until the middle of the twentieth century, kayaks were essential to the survival of the Inuit. A hunter had to own a kayak and know how to use it before he could marry and start a family. Kayaks were so important that they were treated with almost religious respect. Each kayak was custom-made for one hunter who watched over its construction very carefully.

Kayaks were essential to the survival of the Inuit.

Building the Kayak

There are many types of kayaks, but they are all alike in certain ways. They are long (eight to thirty feet), narrow (one and a half to three feet), and shallow (nine inches to two feet). They have pointed ends and watertight, covered decks. In the center of the kayak, between the decks, is a hole slightly larger than the kayaker's waist. Kayakers enter their boats by sliding their legs into the hole and (unlike canoers, who kneel) stretching them out under the forward deck as they

9

Kayaks are extremely light and fast.

sit down. Kayaks do not have keels (the spine that runs along the bottom of the boat), so they turn easily, and they are extremely lightweight. Most Inuit kayaks were so light that hunters could carry their boats on their heads. This meant they could cross the ice out to the open water or walk overland from one inlet to another carrying their kayaks.

In addition to being light and fast, kayaks had to be strong enough to handle heavy Arctic seas. There were few big trees in the far north, so boatbuilders often used driftwood found on beaches to make kayak frames. To make a kayak, the builders first constructed the frame for the deck.

They bent two long pieces of wood so that they met at the ends and curved apart in the middle. These were the gunwales. They secured the gunwales with wooden or bone pegs and rawhide cords. Then they bent wooden ribs to make the curve of the boat's hull or underside. They inserted these ribs into holes in the bottoms of the gunwales. Then they scraped seal or caribou hides completely clean of hair to make the hull. They spread the hides tightly over the frame and sewed waterproof seams with braided sinew, which is animal tendon used like thread. The skin of a kayak in regular use in the extreme cold of the Arctic had to be oiled every four to eight days and changed entirely every year or two.

Kayaks of Different Tribes

The kayaks of different tribes of Inuit peoples varied according to use. The Inuit of Baffin Island, northern Quebec, and Labrador used their kayaks to hunt in the open sea. They needed kayaks that were steady in high swells. As a result, they made wide, heavy kayaks with flat bottoms.

The Copper, Netsilik, and Caribou Inuit of the Central Canadian Arctic hunted swimming caribou in inland lakes and rivers. They built their kayaks for speed. These kayaks were narrow and had rounded hulls. Some had long, pointed horns on the bow (front) and stern (back). These horns provided handholds for rescuers in case a kayak capsized, or tipped over.

The Mackenzie Inuit of the Western Canadian Arctic used their kayaks in the Mackenzie River and Delta. Their boats were similar to the Central Canadian Arctic kayaks, but they tended to be smaller, with ridged decks and upright end horns.

The Inuit used kayaks for hunting caribou in lakes and rivers.

Inuit kayakers generally used two paddle blades joined by one shaft to paddle their boats. They paddled with a continuous, figure-eight arm motion. This was much faster than switching from side to side with a single paddle. It also gave them better control when they wanted to roll their kayaks.

The Eskimo Roll
Rolling is when a kayaker capsizes and then rights the boat without getting out of it. There are several kinds of rolls. Kayakers today call these moves Eskimo rolls. Inuit hunters who rolled wore watertight jackets that fastened directly to

the rims of the holes in their kayaks. This allowed them to roll into the icy Arctic without getting water in their boats.

Not all Inuit kayakers rolled their kayaks, but in some places, the combination of rough water and dangerous hunting made rolling necessary. For kayakers in these regions, rolling was an important skill. Sometimes, during a hunt, a harpoon line could tangle and capsize a boat. Sometimes an injured animal attacked a hunter and tipped the boat over. The kayaker needed to be able to roll the boat back up. The Greenland Inuit were masters of the roll. They paddled narrow kayaks in tricky waters and developed many types of rolls. They could roll their boats using their paddles, their harpoon shafts, or just their hands.

Traditional Kayaking Today

Today, many of the skills of traditional kayaking have been lost. Modern advances and manufactured goods make kayaking less necessary to Inuit life. In addition, many of the animals the Inuit hunted have been overhunted and are now endangered. The kayak, the "hunter's boat," can no longer serve its original purpose.

Traditional kayaking lives on as an art form and a sport. As recently as 1965, one of the most basic motions of the traditional roll, the hip snap, was rediscovered. Kayaking schools in Greenland continue to teach what is known of the methods of the Inuit kayakers. And all over the world, weekend paddlers glide across lakes, heave through ocean swells, and shoot down rivers in canvas and fiberglass boats that are models of the original skin-and-driftwood kayaks of the Inuit.

Kayaking requires strength and endurance.

Good for the Mind and the Body

Kayaking is a sport that requires strength and endurance, and it is a great workout. However, it is not only good for your body; it's also good for your mind and spirit. Like other outdoor sports, kayaking can teach you a lot about yourself. Whether you're trekking across a wide stretch of open water or battling raging rapids, you're becoming smarter, wiser, better. You're meeting challenges, overcoming obstacles, and working as a team with your fellow paddlers.

In recent years, more people than ever have begun to recognize the mental and spiritual value of outdoor activity. Doctors and counselors are encouraging people with physical disabilities and emotional problems to find power and strength in nature. In some places, judges are sending at-risk teens and juvenile offenders to wilderness programs as alternatives to imprisonment.

2 The Right Stuff

Like many cool pursuits, kayaking demands a lot of equipment. In fact, kayaking blows away pretty much any other sport for the pure, high-tech appeal of its stuff.

To be a real kayaker, you need a boat, a paddle, a personal flotation device (PFD), a helmet, and a spray skirt. For anything more hard-core than a day trip on a calm body of

Kayaking requires the right equipment, such as a paddle and helmet.

water, you may also want to look into waterproof packing and flotation bags, bilge pumps, paddle floats, sea socks, weather radios, compasses, global positioning systems (GPS), and emergency signaling devices. You'll learn more about these a little later. If you intend to kayak often, you may also want to get a shiny kayak rack for the roof of your (or your parents') car.

The Boat

First things first: the boat. All kayaks are basically the same. The hull of a kayak is a closed tube with a pointed bow and stern. The boat is slightly wider than a person's hips and the main opening is a hole in the middle of the top for the kayaker to shimmy into.

The two major subgroups of kayaks are sea kayaks and

The modern fiberglass kayak

Paddling out through the surf

whitewater kayaks. The sea kayak is a long, stable boat designed for lakes, quiet rivers, and ocean touring. The whitewater kayak is smaller and shorter. It fits your body more tightly and turns very easily. The whitewater kayak allows its more fearless paddlers (or wearers) to perform wild aquabatics in crashing river rapids. The extreme end of this spectrum is the "squirt boat." Even shorter and smaller than the whitewater kayak, the squirt boat can "squirt" forth—sometimes in a controlled spin and sometimes in a total panic—from the black depths of the most dangerous rapids.

Basic Boat Mechanics

Rather than buying a boat immediately, it is a good idea to rent and borrow as many types and brands as possible. This will help you develop a feel for what you like best. There are some basic guidelines: larger, longer boats are harder to capsize and are faster for straight-ahead travel. Smaller boats are less stable but are more maneuverable and a better bet for the trickier bits of river runs.

It is also a good idea to look at many boats closely and to start to understand how shape affects performance. In addition to size and length, stability is also due to rocker. Rocker is

The kayak can be precisely controlled even in rough water.

the amount of curve along the keel. Touring kayaks have flatter keels. This helps keep them going in one direction. Whitewater boats have more rocker, or curve, to their keels. The bow and stern of a whitewater kayak are, on average, six inches higher than the part of the hull in the middle of the boat beneath the seated kayaker. This makes it much easier to turn.

Picture the raised ends of the boat skidding right or left across the surface of the water, rather than plowing through it underneath the surface. This is very useful when you are trying to avoid a huge boulder looming in the middle of a fast-moving river. The downside is that the more rocker a boat has, and the easier it is to turn, the less stable it is.

Stability is also affected by flare and chine. If you cut a piece-of-bread slice or cross-section out of the middle of a kayak, it would look more or less oval. The cross-sections of some kayaks flare so that they look wider at the top where they touch the waterline. The more flare a boat has, the more stable it is. The cross-sections of some boats are squarish instead of perfectly oval. This is chine. The more chine a boat has, the more stable it is. Whitewater kayaks generally have little or no flare or chine. They are easy to capsize but also easy to roll back up. Sea kayaks have both flare and chine and tend to keep their paddlers drier.

Choosing a Boat

Most sea kayaks are made of fiberglass or plastic. The overall best bet, looking at cost, weight, and durability, is probably plastic. Plastic boats are nearly indestructible. Plastic is relatively inexpensive and comes in a range of styles. It is heavy (it weighs about ten percent more than fiberglass), but if you plan to spend all your time in the water, weight doesn't matter. If you plan to do a lot of "portaging"—carrying your boat overland from one water site to another—weight will be a larger part of your decision.

If you are willing to spend about twenty percent more, fiberglass boats are more beautiful than plastic ones, and they make less noise in the water. This may not matter in crashing rapids, but it is lovely to glide through a silent inlet in a fiberglass kayak. However, if you do opt for a fiberglass boat, remember that fiberglass needs more maintenance.

If you are a whitewater kayaker, you will find that nowadays—except in the case of very specialized squirt boats—almost all whitewater kayaks are plastic. If your primary

You will be drenched but energized after a great river run.

interest is in running rivers, you will want a general-purpose plastic riverboat. If you are more interested in doing stunts and routines, you may need a more specialized "rodeo" play boat.

The Paddle

Now that you have a boat, you need a paddle. Choosing the right paddle is almost as important as choosing the right boat, but it is a much less expensive decision. In fact, like many people, you may want a second, emergency paddle that is completely different from your main paddle.

The Inuit developed the double-bladed kayaking paddle—one shaft or handle with a paddle blade at each end—so they could paddle continuously, without having to switch sides. There have been several changes to paddle construction since the Inuit days, but the main features of a good paddle are

still weight, strength, and balance.

One post-Inuit advance is feathering. A feathered paddle has angled blades; as you hold one blade flat and look along the shaft, the other is anywhere from a few degrees slanted to fully vertical. When you stroke with a feathered paddle, as one blade pulls through the water, the other slices edge-forward through the air and knifes back into the water as your motion twists the shaft. This is marvelous in strong wind, when the flat side of an unfeathered paddle can catch the air like a sail.

Modern kayak paddles

22

There are many small, personal choices about paddles. Paddle blades are either flat or curved like a spoon. Flat blades are convenient because you can paddle with either side. Spooned blades grab the water better and move through it faster. Large blades push against more water; smaller blades offer more control. Oval paddle shafts fit nicely in your hands and force you to hold the paddle correctly. A round shaft allows you to rotate the paddle more easily.

Wooden paddles are traditional and beautiful; wooden shafts have a nice, flexible give and never get too cold to handle. However, they tend to be expensive, and they demand extra care. If you don't mind doing without looks and warmth, fiberglass is durable, less expensive, and flexible. Carbon fiber, Kevlar, and graphite are light and durable, but very expensive.

Some paddles are made in two pieces. This enables you to take them apart for storage. You can also change the amount of feather when you put them back together. Paddlers often choose to use take-apart paddles as their spares. They bungee-cord them in two pieces to the decks of their sea kayaks or store them underneath the deck of white-water boats.

Choose your paddle length according to your height, the length of your arms, the type of boat you have, and how you paddle it. You will want a shorter shaft and narrower blades for fast, whitewater paddling, and a longer shaft and more generously sized blades for long trips across wide stretches of flat water. Try as many types and shapes as you can before you make a decision. Remember, there is nothing more exhausting than battling with a too-long paddle in too-strong wind at the end of a long day.

The Personal Flotation Device

Kayaking is highly entertaining and easy to love, but like all water sports, it can be dangerous. No matter how well you swim, no matter how warm the water, no matter how short the distance from your kayak to the shore, you will need a life jacket.

Unlike the orange neck pillows you may remember hating, the kayaker's personal flotation device or PFD is actually a cool piece of boating gear. Its short cut allows the kayaker to twist freely at the waist. It allows for differences in male and female anatomy. It comes in every imaginable color. Pick the one you like, but remember that safety is more important than appearance or comfort.

When you buckle on a good PFD, it will feel secure around your body and not like it will rise over your head. Do up every buckle, zipper, and waist tie and tighten them; if you leave the PFD open in the front, it won't work. When you do take it off at the beach to eat lunch, tie it down. The last thing you—or your traveling companions—want is to have to hike out from the middle of a fantastic river because you've lost your PFD to a sudden wind.

Helmets are safety essentials.

The Spray Skirt

The spray skirt is what makes your boat a true kayak. It is the piece of coated nylon or neoprene that keeps waves from spilling over your coaming, the curved lip around the edge of the cockpit, into the inside of your boat. It keeps you dry if you capsize, and it allows you to perform an Eskimo roll, which is how you roll your boat back upright from an upside-down position without getting out. The spray skirt also keeps you warm.

Nylon spray skirts are moderately priced and are good for moderate conditions. Neoprene skirts are more expensive and more watertight. They will keep you warmer in the cold or boil you alive in summer heat. If you plan to kayak in cold weather, you should take into account the extra thickness of winter clothes when you measure yourself for a spray skirt.

A leisurely paddle through cold waters can be relaxing.

Generally, though, tighter is better. No one likes cold water seeping into the cockpit.

Spray skirts attach with a plastic cord or elastic band and should fit you and your boat snugly enough to keep you dry. They should not fit so tightly that they can't be pulled off in an emergency. If you plan to roll frequently, you will need a spray skirt designed to handle rough conditions.

3 More Gear

Now you've got the basics: a boat, a paddle, a personal flotation device (PFD), and a spray skirt. Before you set out, however, there are a few more pieces of equipment you may want to consider.

You will need a spare paddle. Breaking a paddle is rare. Not having a spare can be a disaster. Even if you never capsize, you may lose a paddle to a campsite flood or, if it's wooden, to an obnoxious beaver. A take-apart model is easy to strap to your deck or slide behind your seat. Getting a spare paddle is a good opportunity to pick a paddle of different length or blade size from your main paddle.

Ocean boaters might also consider a paddle leash made from thin nylon line

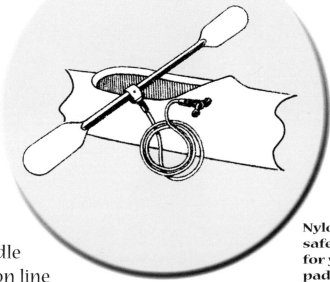

Nylon safety line for your paddle

or elastic cord that connects your paddle either to your wrist or to the deck of your boat. Another paddle accessory is a drip ring. Drip rings are rubber rings that slide onto the shaft of your paddle and prevent water from running down the shaft onto your hands and arms. A paddle float is an inflatable bag that fits onto the blade of your paddle. If you capsize, you can inflate it, attach it to your paddle, and use the combination as a float to support your climb back into the boat. Paddle floats are effective, easy to stow, quite inexpensive, and essential for the solo sea paddler.

Bilge pump

You may also want a bilge pump. If you plan to paddle solo far from land on the open sea, you will need one. Bilge pumps bail the water out of a righted or swamped boat. They can be electric or manual; the electric ones are fast, heavy, and expensive, and do all the work for you. The handheld, manual pumps are light and inexpensive, require some elbow grease, and are more appropriate for kayaks.

Staying Afloat

Kayaks need flotation at both ends. Sea kayaks have built-in compartments, or bulkheads, in the bow and stern where boaters store camping gear or lunch. Others use air bags in front of the feet and behind the seat. Flotation is particularly

Universal River Signals

Knowing the commonly understood river signals is a critical part of water safety. A river is a loud and complicated place. When you cannot make yourself heard above the roar of the whitewater, you will need to know how to talk with your paddle.

- If you are paddling stick (going first) and want the people behind you to portage the hair-raising drop you just barely survived: Raise your paddle and rest it on top of your shoulder.

- If you are in an emergency or need help: Wave your paddle, helmet, or PFD over your head in a circular motion.

- To tell other paddlers to stop: Raise your paddle horizontally above your head and make a pumping motion, or stick out your arms and flap like a bird.

- If you want your worried fellow paddlers to know that you are okay: Raise your open hand above your head and pat yourself on the helmet.

- If everything is fine, and you want the paddlers behind you to follow you straight down the middle of the river: Hold your paddle straight above your head with its face toward them.

- If everything is fine, and you want the paddlers behind you to follow you to one side or the other: Angle your paddle toward the desired route.

- Remember: Never point toward an obstacle—the people watching you will kayak straight into it.

(Signals established by the American Canoe Association.)

important in a boat loaded with camping equipment.

For long, open crossings on lakes or oceans, boaters without bulkheads often use sea socks. These are large, coated nylon bags that fit into the hull and tie around the coaming. You sit inside the sock inside the kayak and secure your spray skirt on the coaming over it. A sea sock doesn't provide the buoyancy of bulkheads or air bags, but it does reduce the amount of water that can come on board if you capsize.

If you plan to do anything longer than a day trip, you will need nylon or vinyl waterproof dry bags to store gear in your boat. These are not flotation bags, but they do aid buoyancy because the more space they take up—crammed full of food and equipment—the less space there is for water to fill when you capsize. Nylon is lighter, easier to pack, less apt to tear, and doesn't stiffen in cold weather. Vinyl is less expensive. Dry bags are usually referred to by color and size. "Hey, grab Big Red, will you?" or "Toss over Little Yellow."

Navigation

One of the most important things to consider when embarking on a wilderness adventure is how not to get lost. It is generally hard to lose your way on a river. But sea and lake kayakers should carry a compass, a device that magnetically determines geographical direction. Small, inexpensive, hiking compasses are perfectly adequate if you know how to use them. (Using a compass may be trickier than you think; talk to your kayaking instructor or someone at the sporting goods store before embarking on your trip.) There are also big, heavy, waterproof marine compasses that attach to your boat and provide readings of the direction of your bow.

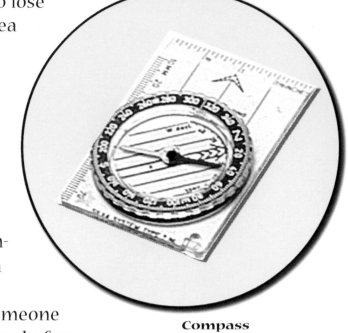

Compass

Much cooler than a compass—and significantly more expensive—is the global positioning system, or GPS. This is a small, handheld, battery-operated device that triangulates your position by satellite. You can use it to pinpoint your position anywhere on earth to within about a hundred yards. It is particularly useful in fog, on overcast nights, or for long, open crossings where boaters have to take compass readings almost constantly.

Safety

Unless you are perfecting your Eskimo roll in a swimming pool, or paddling within shouting distance of the Coast Guard, you will need some emergency signaling devices. The most basic is a flare, which produces a bright light for signaling. There are several kinds of flares. Meteor flares send a rocket up several hundred feet and continue to burn while they fall. Parachute flares use a small parachute to keep the light aloft. Handheld flares are useful on flat, open water and last for about two minutes.

You can also purchase a strobe light or a signal mirror. Strobe lights are battery-powered and highly visible by day and night. They can also be tested, unlike flares, and can be turned off to save power when no rescuer is in sight. In sunny weather, nothing catches the eye of a search and rescue pilot like the flash of a signal mirror.

A major piece of safety equipment for the whitewater kayaker is the throw rope. A throw rope enables you to pull another struggling or capsized kayaker out of a tricky place in a river. It is important to learn how to use a throw rope correctly from an instructor or advanced boater. If you throw a rope without bracing (supporting) it, you may be pulled into a dangerous river by the kayaker you are trying to save. If you brace it incorrectly around your arm or leg, you may cut off your own circulation. Once you know how to use a throw rope, you should carry it with you whenever you are scouting rapids from a river bank. You never know when a friend or stranger may need your help.

What to Wear

The number-one choice in cold-weather, water sport garb for sailors and kayakers is the drysuit. A drysuit is a tight-fitting suit that will actually keep you completely dry from neck to wrists to ankles even when fully submerged in ice-cold water. The drawback is that it can be constricting to wear one in a kayak. Riverboaters tend to wear dry tops, which keep them dry and warm from the waist up while their legs stay warm beneath their kayak skirts.

The next choice is the wetsuit. A wetsuit—like the sturdier spray skirts   is made of neoprene. It fits snugly against your body but is not watertight. When you capsize, it traps a thin film of water against your skin. Warmed by your body heat, this layer of water becomes an incredibly effective layer of insulation.

Wetsuits range from neck-to-wrist-to-ankle outfits to sleeveless vests called "farmer Johns" that allow kayakers full freedom to move their arms.

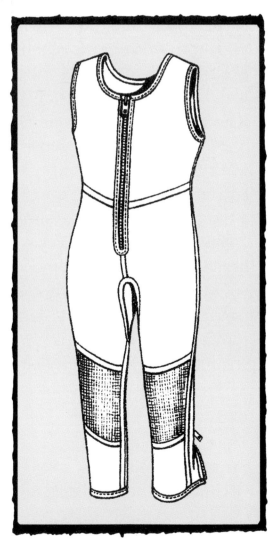

If you don't plan to kayak in cold spring water (or you hate to shop), you may already own everything you need. Desirable materials include wool and synthetics like Lycra or polypropylene. Water runs right out of these fabrics, and they keep you warm even when they're wet. Cotton T-shirts are not good because they hold water rather than draining it off— if you've ever been pushed into a pool you may have noticed this.

Neoprene wet suit

It is always wise to layer. If you buy only one kayak-specific piece of clothing, you might pick a paddling jacket or loose pullover of treated nylon. Unlike the average windbreaker, paddling jackets are designed with neoprene closures at the neck and wrists to keep the water out.

You might also want to consider buying paddling gloves, because wet skin blisters easily. For cold weather, you can wear pogies, special mittens that attach to the shaft of your paddle. You will definitely need thick-soled sneakers or nylon sandals to protect your feet from rocky lake and river bottoms. (Remember: When spilled into fast-moving water, you should keep your feet up and pointed downstream and let your rubber soles and rump bump off the rocks. Never stand in moving water; you might catch your foot between two rocks and break your leg.)

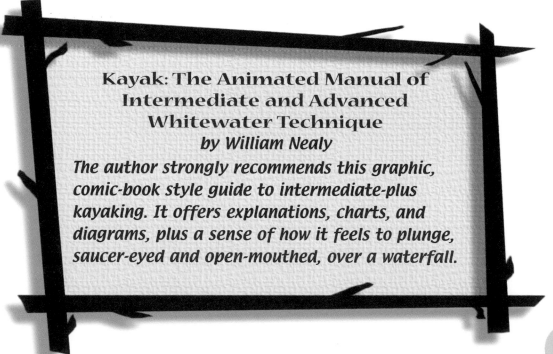

Kayak: The Animated Manual of Intermediate and Advanced Whitewater Technique
by William Nealy
The author strongly recommends this graphic, comic-book style guide to intermediate-plus kayaking. It offers explanations, charts, and diagrams, plus a sense of how it feels to plunge, saucer-eyed and open-mouthed, over a waterfall.

One Last Word

Although it is important to have safe, high-quality equipment, there's no need to go crazy right up front. You have years of kayaking ahead of you. There's plenty of time to figure out what you like.

Proper paddling technique saves energy.

4 Now You're Paddling

Now that you have all your gear, it is time to find the most important thing of all: a qualified paddling instructor or an experienced friend or family member. Learning from someone who knows what he or she is doing will help you learn the right skills safely and in the right order. It will prevent you from developing bad habits, provide you with someone to answer your questions, and make sure you have someone to guide you through the tricky bits.

Kayaking in groups is safer.

If you don't have access to an instructor, or don't know any kayakers, check out the opportunities for learning how to kayak at your school, at nearby colleges, or through the YMCA or local youth groups. Some retail stores offer lessons, as do kayaking clubs. You can also learn a lot from books and videos, but—no matter how good the book or video—it is dangerous to go out onto the water to try to teach yourself to paddle.

Getting in the Boat

First—obviously!—you have to get into the boat. Step into your spray skirt while still on dry land, pull it up above your waist, and roll it up a little so it doesn't interfere with your legs. The most important thing to remember when climbing into any boat is to keep your weight low. Put your kayak into shallow water, grip your paddle shaft in one hand and press it flat across the rear of the cockpit. Use your other hand to hold the shaft just beyond the side of the boat with one blade resting on the shore for support. The even pressure from your hands should hold the boat steady. Step into the middle of the cockpit with one foot, sit carefully on the back deck, and pull in the other foot. Now, with your arms still behind you, slide over the paddle and down into the cockpit.

As your weight drops from waist-height to ankle-height, the boat will suddenly feel much more secure. Now bring your paddle around, balance it across the front deck, and secure your spray skirt. It is generally easiest to start in the back, then attach the front, and finish with the sides. You will now feel very cozy. You may also be worried about ever getting out of this thing in the terrifying event that you capsize. Fortunately, there is a grab loop at the front of the

Some sporting goods stores provide information on kayaking clubs.

skirt. Try pulling it forward and up and then toward you.
Instantly the whole thing will release.

More than anything, you should feel that you are
wearing the kayak. It should fit you like a good pair of jeans:
not tight, but snug, and able to move with you as smoothly
as part of your own body. When you are in your kayak, you
should check the fit for your feet, knees, thighs, seat, back,
and hips. Your feet will rest against a pair of pedals or a flat
platform that adjusts to your height. A pair of padded
braces holds your knees and thighs, and the seat, backrest,

and foam hip pads should hold your body firmly without cramping your movement.

And You're Off!

So here you are, wrapped in your kayak and ready to go. Time to pick up the paddle. Your main hand—the left for lefties and right for righties—is your "control" hand. The other is your "slip" hand. With your control hand, hold the paddle shaft

Your main paddling hand—left if you're a lefty, and right if you're a righty—is your "control" hand.

about a fist's width from the top of the blade. Keep your wrist straight and pull the blade through the water. As it rises behind you, stroke down with your slip hand. Your control hand should always be firm on the paddle. Your slip hand should loosen between strokes so you can rotate the paddle and face the blade squarely to the water.

The correct motion here is box-like: first cock one wrist back by your shoulder, punch out with the paddle, and then stroke down and back. Concentrate on pushing the shaft out with your upper hand, rather than pulling back with the lower hand. One of the advantages of the double-bladed paddle is that you can use this stronger pushing force directly from your shoulder to power the boat.

Your instructor may start you off by standing beside your boat in calm, waist-deep water. To get a feel for the way the boat rests in the water, she may suggest that you rock the boat from side to side. It is very important to be able to feel loose in the kayak and to let it rock under you. The looser you are at the waist, the more stable and secure your kayak will feel. Your instructor will help you hold the boat down to the right for a few seconds and then bring it upright with a snap of your hips. This hip-snap is the basis for the Eskimo roll.

She may also ask you to try a wet exit. A wet exit is when you slide out of your capsized boat underwater. First you have to capsize. Before you tip over, make sure there are no rocks under you. Now, hold on to your paddle and throw your weight to one side of the boat until you pull it over. (This is called turtling the boat because the upturned hull looks like the shell of a turtle.)

You are now hanging upside down from your boat in the water. Slide your control hand to the middle of your

Your instructor may have you try a wet exit.

paddle. Use your slip hand to pull the grab loop on your skirt. When it comes free, grip the sides of the cockpit with your hands (your control hand is still holding the paddle), push back and up, and force yourself away from the boat. After some initial resistance, you will shoot away from the boat and your PFD will pull you to the surface.

The first time you do this, your instructor will probably let you tow your boat to shore and get back in the easy way. However, you do need to learn how to right your boat and get back in from the water—with or without help.

Strokes and Braces

Now that you are prepared for the worst, it's time to learn to enjoy yourself. First you need to learn to paddle. Paddling breaks down into four major types of strokes. Although these blend to the untrained eye, they are quite distinct and have particular uses. The power stroke pulls you forward. The forward sweep pushes the boat forward and turns it away from the paddle side. The reverse sweep pushes the boat back and turns it away from the paddle side. The draw pulls the boat toward the paddle.

Sea kayakers and whitewater kayakers both use all of these strokes. However, touring is mainly about paddling, or moving the boat through still water, while river kayaking is also about keeping the boat stable in moving water. To hold a

There are four major types of kayaking strokes: power, forward sweep, reverse sweep, and draw.

whitewater kayak stable in "squirrelly" water, you need to learn to brace. Bracing is a technique for holding a paddle in the water to stabilize a kayak.

There are low braces and high braces. In the low brace, you hold yourself and your kayak upright by rotating your wrists down and pressing the back side of the paddle onto the water. Just like when you belly flop and smack against the hard surface of the pool, your paddle will resist sinking into the water. In this way, you can use the surface of the water to stabilize yourself.

In the high brace, you raise your arms, stick your paddle into the water, and press the paddle face against a flat surface of water underwater. The high brace feels less secure than the low brace because lifting your arm so high raises your center of gravity (this is why the boat feels less stable when you stand). It is also dangerous because it can put enough pressure on your arms to dislocate your shoulder. The high brace is most useful when your boat is already tipped way over. It is generally considered an emergency brace. You should use the much safer low brace to try to prevent these emergencies.

Ready to Roll

If you catch on quickly and express an interest, perhaps you'll move right into the Eskimo roll. After all, you have already mastered the basic elements: the high and low brace and a gentle version of the hip snap.

Your need for a foolproof roll will vary with the type of kayaking you do. Many sea and lake kayakers never roll at all. On the other hand, there are unplanned situations in which a roll will save even the most cautious kayaker from a cold or dangerous swim. River wisdom dictates that, once over, you should keep trying to "roll till you puke," to avoid that swim.

Be ready to roll because it will happen!

A successful Eskimo roll depends upon the power of the hips. To practice, paddle your kayak into waist-deep water at the lip of a pool or next to a friend or instructor. Lean over and hold the pool edge or person's hands. Flip yourself and your boat until you are as close to upside down as you can get with your cheek just resting on the surface of the water so you can breathe. Now, focus all your strength into your hips.

The hip-snap flicks your body like a whip. Power moves up from your hips and along your side and yanks your shoulders, neck, and head out of the water—but only after the boat is righted. A strong whip curves like an arch. If you try to pull your head up first—which is tempting because you want to breathe— the whip shape will collapse and your boat will re-turtle. This is because your hip muscles are strong enough to lift your head, but

Try paddling for speed!

your neck muscles cannot lift your whole body and your kayak. It is best to practice this motion many times. Keep turtling and righting your boat over and over while keeping your cheek resting, unmoving, on the surface of the pool. This motion will also teach you to keep your waist loose, which lets the kayak ride out bumps on the river and keeps it much more stable.

Most kayakers use the screw roll as their basic (or combat) roll. In the screw roll, your body bends diagonally forward over the front of the boat. To practice the screw roll, lean your weight against the beam of the boat until you capsize; now you are upside down in the water. To come back up, place your paddle flat against the surface, pull across the surface, and snap your hips., bringing your head up last.

The other basic survival roll is called the C-to-C, which brings you up over the bow. Whichever you prefer, it is important to have a totally reliable roll that will get you up even "in traffic," no matter how rough or complicated the water around you is.

Showing Off Your Roll

Once your hip snap is perfect, you will be able to learn to hand roll. In a hand roll, you substitute the motion of your hand for the motion of your paddle and pull the boat around almost entirely with your body. Hand rolling is more than a stunt. Kayak-polo players often lose their paddles and capsize when shooting goals. On rough rivers a kayaker in trouble can sometimes use a hand roll to reach the bank or retrieve a dropped paddle.

Finally, there is the all-important "Coke roll," in which the paddler—who must be able to roll one-handed—holds a full and open Coke can in his right hand and, while capsizing to the left, sets it on the upturned hull. His left hand then comes under the boat from the other side and, as the boat rolls up, retrieves the still-full can. This roll won't save you from drowning, but it will definitely impress your friends.

Playing Stick and Paddling Sweep

One way to test the speed and direction of whitewater is to toss sticks into it and make sure they "live." As a result, the kayaker who braves the first run describes her job as "playing stick."

Usually one of the two most experienced kayakers on a trip plays stick, while the other most experienced paddler "sweeps." This means he brings up the rear and keeps counting heads to make sure no one gets left behind.

Beyond including a strong first and last paddler, every kayaking trip should have a clear group rescue plan. Every member of the trip should have some basic rescue skills, understand how to use a throw rope, and know the basics for getting to swimmers. Getting to swimmers quickly is probably the most important part of keeping a kayaking outing safe.

5 Into the Wild World of Kayaking

Kayaking can take you to some of the most beautiful places on earth.

Perfecting your screw roll is about as exciting as it gets in your next-door neighbor's swimming pool. Now it's time to hit the real water. One of the great beauties of kayaking, and a major reason so many people do it and love it, is that it takes you to some of the most beautiful places in the world. It also allows you to see them from an angle—sea level, really close up—

that even natives never get to see them from. Some of these places, like Myanmar or the South Pole, are worth keeping in mind for future outings, but you will be amazed by how many fantastic kayaking destinations are right in your own backyard.

If you want to start small and local, you can probably think of water no more than a mile from where you live. Maybe you live near the ocean; maybe there's a big swimming lake in your town; maybe you're near a slow, flat section of a river in which you could get some good, solid practice before hitting serious whitewater. If nothing comes to mind, look in the phone book or ask your parents or your friends. There are state parks and national preserves all over the country that offer recreational boating for people with or without their own equipment. You may be surprised how much kayaking action is no more than a bike ride away.

If kayaking sounds appealing, but you aren't sure you're ready for the Eskimo roll, you might want to start with a guided tour. A guided tour is a relaxed, scenery-oriented glide that will give you a taste of the river without pushing you into the drink. You should also find out if there is a paddling club near you. A paddling club could provide you with news and information about paddling in your area, introductions to fellow paddlers, and a chance to rent or borrow gear before investing in your own.

Before you go, though, remember this. Although there is always the opportunity to push yourself, this does not mean you should behave irresponsibly or attempt something that frightens you. Be sure to consult the International Scale of River Difficulty for any whitewater run you attempt.

Kayaking Competitively

If you want to kayak competitively, there are three general categories of kayaking games. Each demands the capabilities of a boater at a strong intermediate level or better. The most grueling is the down-river slalom race. This type of race tends to be ten miles or more and requires highly developed river-reading skills as well as strong upper-body muscles. Your task is to choose the most efficient path through the course and finish in the shortest time.

Once you have mastered the sport, you may want to kayak competitively.

The International Scale of River Difficulty
(according to the American Whitewater Affiliation)

Class I (pre-beginner). Class I water is fast and smooth with obvious obstructions that are easy to avoid. It poses little danger for swimmers, and spilled kayakers will not need assistance to recover themselves and their boats.

Class II (beginner). Class II is faster and includes more rocks and waves, but it offers visually obvious routes and does not demand scouting from the banks. Swimmers are generally able to rescue themselves.

Class III (intermediate). Class III runs include rocks and ledges that require quick turns and maneuvers. Truly dangerous rocks or waves are avoidable, but the strength of the water demands good boat control. Inexperienced boaters should scout Class III water before running it. Party members should be prepared to offer group help to swimmers.

Class IV (advanced intermediate). Class IV water may include unavoidable holes, large waves, or narrow stretches between rocks and ledges. Kayakers may be forced to execute strong, fast turns to avoid obstructions or cross eddy lines. (An eddy is the still or slow-moving area of water behind a protecting feature like a rock.) Boating parties need to scout Class IV sections before running them. Given the level of risk for swimmers, kayakers should attempt these runs only with a practiced Eskimo roll.

Class V (expert). Class V water is for experts. It includes long stretches of violent water, steep drops, and narrow, complex passages. The consistency of the difficulty requires both physical strength and endurance. Class V water must be scouted each time it is run, although it may include sections that are tricky to view from the bank. The risks for swimmers are significant.

Class VI (extreme and exploratory). Class VI runs push the envelope even for experts. They are technically challenging, unpredictable, and may never have been run before. The force of the water or sheer sides of the river canyon may make rescuing swimmers impossible.

Slalom and rodeo courses are featured at kayak competitions.

Slalom-gate courses are short, usually about 50 yards long, and related to slalom skiing courses in their use of "gates." The kayaker runs the gates—which occur among and around various tricky bits of whitewater—in a particular order that sometimes involves a fair amount of backpaddling. Contestants are judged for time and lose points for missing or touching gates as well as for running them out of order.

The hotdogger's version of competitive kayaking is rodeo. A rodeo "course" is a water feature like the hole at the bottom of a drop. Sometimes a contest involves specific moves. Sometimes people use their imaginations—they do airborne somersaults or spin upside down or juggle fruit. Since 1993, the rodeo circuit has gotten more serious. One of the reasons for this is the speed with which boat technology

Breaking the Falls

On July 31, 1998, twenty-year-old competitive kayaker Shannon Carroll ran the 78-foot Sahalie Falls, on Eugene, Oregon's McKenzie River. When Shannon saw Sahalie Falls, she knew that she wanted to run it. She tested the water by rolling logs over the top and watching what happened to them. She saw that they went deep into the pool below the falls and then surfaced a short distance downstream. She figured that she could follow that path in her kayak. She checked for dangerous rock protrusions on the cliff behind the falls and found that it was smooth. She was sure that she could run it.

Always a daredevil, Shannon has run numerous falls and won many rodeo and extreme competitions. Within forty-five minutes of first seeing Sahalie, Shannon was ready to go. Today she is the world-record holder, among men and women, for an all-vertical run of a natural waterfall.

is improving. The moves possible in today's boats would have been impossible ten years ago. Rodeo used to mean a bunch of very good stunt kayakers showing off; today it means complex and demanding moves linked into ballet-like routines.

Whatever type and level of kayaking you pursue, there is plenty of room and plenty of opportunity to push yourself or not, exactly as you choose. From the Inuit hunter to the extreme squirt boater to the weekend paddler, the kayak is a boat for all people in all times. It is the only boat that makes us at one with the sea.

A maneuver like this is for experts only!

Glossary

Beam
The width of a kayak at its widest point.

Bow
The front of a boat.

Brace
A technique for holding a paddle in the water to stabilize a kayak.

Bulkhead
A sealed compartment in the bow or stern of a kayak used for storage and flotation.

Coaming
The curved lip around the edge of the cockpit.

Draw stroke
A paddle stroke that pulls or pushes a boat sideways.

Eddy
The still or slow-moving area of water behind a protecting feature like a rock.

Feathering
Twisting a paddle blade so that its sharp edge cuts through the air.

Hip snap
The strong, hip-first body jerk that allows paddlers to right their capsized kayaks; the basis for the Eskimo roll.

Hole

A circular water feature that can form behind an obstruction and submerge or trap a kayaker.

Hull

The body of a boat.

Kayak

A small enclosed boat propelled by the double-bladed paddle of the (usually) single boater.

Navigation

The process of planning a course and steering a boat from a starting point to a destination.

Obstructions

Rocks or other objects that can block a paddler's path and cause rapids.

Rapids

The foaming whitewater that forms around rocks and underwater obstructions or from contradictory currents.

Roll

The method a kayaker uses to right a kayak without getting out of it.

Stern

The back of a boat.

Sweep Stroke

A paddle stroke whose long bow-to-stern arc turns the boat away from the paddle side.

Resources

Kayaking Organizations

In the United States

American Canoe Association (ACA)
7432 Alban Station Boulevard, Suite B-232
Springfield, VA 22150
(703) 451-0141
Web site: http://www.aca-paddler.org

American Whitewater Affiliation (AWA)
1430 Fenwick Lane
Silver Spring, MD 20910
(301) 589-9453
Web site: http://www.awa.org

National Organization for Rivers (NORS)
212 West Cheyenne Mountain
Colorado Springs, CO 80906
(719) 579-8759
Web site: http://www.nationalrivers.org

National Park Service (NPS)
1849 C Street NW
Washington, DC 20240
(202) 208-6843
Web site: http://www.nps.gov

United States Canoe Association (USCA)
606 Ross Street
Middletown, OH 45044
(513) 422-3739
Web site: http://usca-canoe-kayak.org

In Canada

Canadian Parks and Wilderness Society (CPWS)
880 Wellington Street, Suite 506
Ottawa, ON K1R 6K7
(800) 333-WILD
(613) 569-7226
Web site: http://www.cpaws.org

Canadian Recreational Canoeing Association (CRCA)
446 Main Street West
Merrickville, ON K0G 1N0
(888) 252-6292
(613) 269-2910
Web site: http://www.crca.ca

Wilderness Canoe Association (WCA)
P.O. Box 48022
Davisville Postal Outlet
1881 Yonge Street
Toronto, ON M4S 3C6
Web site: http://www.wildernesscanoe.org

For Further Reading

Books About Kayaking

Dutky, Paul. *The Bombproof Roll and Beyond.* Birmingham, AL: Menasha Ridge Press, 1993.

Dyson, George. *Baidarka: The Kayak.* Portland, OR: Graphic Arts Center, 1994.

Hanson, Jonathan. *Complete Sea Kayak Touring.* New York: McGraw-Hill, 1998.

Harrison, David. Ed. *Whitewater Kayaking.* Mechanicsburg, PA: Stackpole, 1998.

Lewis, Linda. *Water's Edge: Women Who Push the Limits in Rowing, Kayaking, and Canoeing.* Seattle, WA: Seal Press, 1992.

Mohle, Robert. *Adventure Kayaking: Trips from Big Sur to San Diego.* Berkeley, CA: Wilderness Press, 1998.

O'Neill, David and Elizabeth O'Neill. *Paddling Okeefenokee National Wildlife Refuge.* Whitmore Lake, MI: Falcon Publishing, 1998.

Solomon, Gary and Mark Solomon. *The Kayak Express! Getting Off the Ground.* Boston, MA: Aquatics Unlimited, 1998.

Guides for Kayaking Adventures

Cassady, Jim, Bill Cross and Fryar Calhoun. *Western Whitewater from the Rockies to the Pacific: A River Guide for Raft, Kayak, and Canoe.* Berkeley, CA: North Forks Press, 1994.

Penny, Richard. *The Whitewater Sourcebook: A Sourcebook of Information on American Whitewater Rivers.* Birmingham, AL: Menasha Ridge Press, 1997.

Venn, Tamsin. *Sea Kayaking Along the Mid-Atlantic Coast: Coastal Paddling Adventures from New York to Chesapeake Bay.* Boston, MA: Appalachian Mountain Club, 1994.

Index

Credits

About the Author

Allison Stark Draper is a writer and editor who grew up spending summers paddling on a lake in Maine. She lives in New York City and the Catskills.

Photo Credits

Series Design

Oliver H. Rosenberg

Layout

Law Alsobrook